For: _____

Those who love deeply never grow old.
—BENJAMIN FRANKLIN

A heart at peace gives life to the body.
PROVERBS 14:30

From: _____

Quiet Times for Teachers
Copyright 1999 by ZondervanPublishingHouse
ISBN 0-310-98008-9

Requests for information should be addressed to:

Zondervan*Gifts*

Mail Drop B20
Grand Rapids, Michigan 49530
http://www.zondervan.com

Senior Editor: Gwen Ellis
Project Editor: Pat Matuszak
Designed By: Koechel Peterson

Printed in China

99 00 01 /HK/ 4 3 2 1

QUIET TIMES FOR
Teachers

*Inspirational Thoughts
to Refresh Your Spirit*

Zondervan*Gifts*

Introduction

Teacher—it's more than a title. It's a lifestyle—a way of living that shows not only by word, but also by example, a pathway for life. So important is the idea of teacher that it is a name taken by Jesus Christ during his tenure on earth. "Rabbi." "Teacher."

His classroom was not a formal schoolroom, but a hillside overlooking the Sea of Galilee. His lesson plan was not theory and untested ideas. His was the plan of the ages. His plan developed the idea of eternal life. His method encouraged student participation to test his ideas. His communication style was to tell stories that brought hidden truths to light. His demonstrations were signs, miracles, and wonders that backed the claims made in his lectures. His classroom demeanor was both tough and tender. On the one hand, he held children on his lap and taught about heaven, and on the other, he wielded a whip to drive the money changers from the temple and teach about honesty and respect.

He was the perfect example. He was never too severe with those who were ready to admit their faults, nor was he too soft on offenders who were not. His flawless life was the perfect role model for students who hadn't a clue how to live.

He elevated the status of title of "teacher" for all time by becoming a teacher himself. It may be true that the hand that rocks the cradle rules the world, but right after that is the teacher who shapes the mind of impressionable young students and gives them nobility of character, inquiring minds, and the basic skills to pursue any dream they may ever have.

Teacher, hold your head high, for yours is a great and noble profession. We are very grateful for all you are doing to help shape the next generation. Thanks for everything!

Contents

Few professions are more of a proving ground for the concept of faith than teaching. Teachers have faith that it is possible to communicate the most intangible principles to students who are at ages where they are the most tangible of thinkers. Teachers have faith that their influence will somehow draw out the best in the worst of their charges, and that this will become evident to parents who often get rather vague reports from their students about the day's learning experiences. When it comes to knowing God, teachers want a faith that has "legs." They need a faith by which they can walk on into the "lions' den" of board meetings. They want a faith to climb the mountain of essay exam papers that need grading. They want a faith that will carry them all the way through to the end of life.

Chapter One

FAITH

I ♥ my teacher

Lord of my life, saturate me with your rain,

toughen me in the strong winds of your Spirit,

flow me green in the floodlight of our sunshine.

Let me be a shade for someone's fatigue,

and shapely enough for an artist to want

to paint me into her landscape.

May your small birds want to nest in me.

May I be a landmark, a signpost

to those who are confused

or who have lost their way.

– Luci Shaw

God's compassions never fail.
They are new every morning;
great is your faithfulness.
I say to myself,
"The LORD is my portion;
therefore I will wait for him."
The LORD is good
to those whose hope is in him,
to the one who seeks him;
it is good to wait quietly
for the salvation of the LORD.

LAMENTATIONS 3:22-26

He put a new song in my mouth,

a hymn of praise to our God.

Many will see and fear

and put their trust in the LORD.

Blessed is the man

who makes the LORD his trust.

Psalm 40:3-4

LIVES OF GREAT MEN ALL REMIND US
We can make our lives sublime,
And departing, leave behind us
Footprints on the sands of time;

Footprints, that perhaps another,
Sailing o'er life's solemn main,
A forlorn and shipwrecked brother,
Seeing, shall take heart again.

Let us then, be up and doing,
With a heart for any fate;
Still achieving, still pursuing,
Learn to labor and to wait.

—Henry Wadsworth Longfellow

Teach me your way, O LORD,

and I will walk in your truth;

give me an undivided heart,

that I may fear your name.

I will praise you, O Lord my God, with all my heart;

I will glorify your name forever.

For great is your love toward me;

you have delivered me from the depths of the grave.

Psalm 86:11–13

LORD, RESTORE TO ME THE *innocent* WISDOM OF MY *childhood.* TAKE AWAY THE BLINDERS THAT KEEP ME FROM SEEING THAT *life* IS SO MUCH MORE THAN MEETS THE EYE.

What would our daily life look like if it were infused with a sacramental understanding of reality? If we realized that the boundaries between heaven and earth are more like gossamer than steel? If we really believed that God knows what goes on in every home and every heart, wouldn't it make a difference?

When you sit down with your family for dinner, remember that God will be there. No matter how chaotic your evening mealtime might be, ask yourself whether you might be entertaining angels. Perhaps there are a couple sitting nearby, ready to pass along an extra helping of grace just when you need it most.

—*Ann Spangler*

THEN PART THE CURTAIN, JUST A BIT,

AND GIVE ME A *glimpse* OF YOUR *angels*

AT *work* BEHIND THE SCENES.

AMEN.

*L*et the morning bring me word of your unfailing love,

for I have put my trust in you.

Show me the way I should go,

for to you I lift up my soul.

Teach me to do your will,

for you are my God;

may your good Spirit

lead me on level ground.

Psalm 143:8,10

I charge you, in the sight of God and Christ Jesus and the elect

angels, to keep these instructions without partiality.

1 Timothy 5:21

$\mathcal{T}$he foundations of our society and our government rest so much on the teachings of the Bible, that it would be difficult to support them if faith in these teachings would cease to be practically universal in our country.

–Calvin Coolidge

$\mathcal{G}$od's Word, contained in the Bible, has furnished all necessary rules to direct our conduct.

–Noah Webster

> *Seek the LORD*
> *all you humble of the land,*
> *you who do what he commands.*
> *Seek righteousness, seek humility.*
>
> ZEPHANIAH 2:3

For the LORD God is a sun and shield;

the LORD bestows favor and honor;

no good thing does he withhold

from those whose walk is blameless.

Psalm 84:11

I HAVE MYSELF FOR MANY YEARS MADE IT A PRACTICE TO READ THROUGH THE BIBLE ONCE EVERY YEAR. I have always endeavored to read it with the same spirit and temper of mind which I now recommend to you; that is, with the intention and desire that it contribute to my advancement in wisdom and virtue ... My custom is, to read four or five chapters every morning, immediately after rising from my bed. It employs about an hour of my time, and seems to me the most suitable manner of beginning the day.

—John Quincy Adams

Our citizenship is in heaven. And we eagerly await a Savior from there, the Lord Jesus Christ, who, by the power that enables him to bring everything under his control, will transform our lowly bodies so that they will be like his glorious body.

Therefore, my brothers, you whom I love and long for, my joy and crown, that is how you should stand firm in the Lord, dear friends! …Agree with each other in the Lord…Rejoice in the Lord always. I will say it again: Rejoice!

Let your gentleness be evident to all. The Lord is near.

Philippians 3:20—4:2,4–5

We can know God is watching over our lives with love. He is like a parent's blessing hovering over a sleeping child, and he gives us peace. He is aware of our daily needs for time, energy, and strength and will help us rise to the tasks that await us daily.

Those who hope in the LORD

will renew their strength.

They will soar on wings like eagles;

they will run and not grow weary,

they will walk and not be faint.

Isaiah 40:31

God has not left himself without testimony: He has shown kindness by giving you rain from heaven and crops in their seasons; he provides you with plenty of food and fills your hearts with joy.

Acts 14:17

Chapter Two

PEACE

I ♥ my teacher

QUIET TIMES FOR
Teachers

To laugh often and much;
to win the respect of intelligent people
and the affection of children;
to earn the appreciation of honest critics
and endure the betrayal of false friends;
to appreciate beauty,
to find the best in others;
to leave the world a bit better,
whether by a healthy child,
a garden patch,
or a redeemed social condition.
To know even one life has breathed easier
because you have lived;
this is to have succeeded.

—RALPH WALDO EMERSON

*I*mitate those who through faith and
patience inherit what has been promised....
We have this hope as an anchor for the soul,
firm and secure. It enters the inner sanctuary
behind the curtain, where Jesus, who went before
us, has entered on our behalf. He has become
a high priest forever.

Hebrews 6:12, 19-20

*T*HE REAL MYSTERY OF JOHANN SEBASTIAN BACH'S life as a composer concerns how he found the actual time to have created so many masterpieces cherished through the ages. All of his composing took place while he was working as an organist, a conductor, a music director, a private instructor, even a teacher of Latin to young boys— not to mention raising a large family.

At the beginning of his Little Organ Book, Bach wrote this dedication: "To God alone the praise be given for what's herein to man's use written."

—Patrick Kavanaugh

Do not be anxious about anything,

but in everything, by prayer and petition,

with thanksgiving, present your requests to God.

And the peace of God, which transcends all understanding,

will guard your hearts and your minds in Christ Jesus.

Philippians 4:6–7

Come, let us bow down in worship,

let us kneel before the LORD our Maker;

for he is our God

and we are the people of his pasture,

the flock under his care.

Psalm 95:6–7

Thou walkest with me when I walk;

When to my bed for rest I go,

I find thee there,

And everywhere;

Not youngest thought in me doth grow,

No, not one word I cast to talk,

But yet unuttered thou dost know.

If forth I march, thou goest before,

If back I turn, thou comst behind

So forth nor back

Thy guard I lack,

Nay, on me, too, thy hand I find.

Well I thy wisdom may adore,

But never reach with earthy mind.

My God, how I these studies prize

That do thy hidden workings show!

Whose sum is such

No sum so much,

Nay summed as sand, they sumless grow.

I lie to sleep, from sleep I rise,

Yet still in thought with thee I go.

—Mary Herbert

O LORD, you have searched me and you know me.

You know when I sit and when I rise;

    you perceive my thoughts from afar.

You discern my going out and my lying down;

    you are familiar with all my ways.

Before a word is on my tongue you know it completely, O LORD.

You hem me in—behind and before;

    you have laid your hand upon me.

Such knowledge is too wonderful for me,

    too lofty for me to attain.

Psalm 139:1–6

In the Gospels, the Lord Jesus is presented as the Friend of sinners. For historically He was found, first of all, moving among men as their Friend before He became their Savior. But do you realize that today He is still in the first place our Friend, in order that He may become our Savior? Before we have reached the point where we are willing— or indeed able—to receive Him as Savior, He comes to us as a Friend, so that personal encounter is not debarred to us, and the door is held open for us to receive Him as Savior. This is a precious discovery.

—Watchman Nee

WHEN JESUS saw their faith,
he said, "Friend, your sins are forgiven."

Luke 5:20

A MAN OF MANY COMPANIONS
may come to ruin,
but there is a friend
who sticks closer than a brother.

Proverbs 18:24

He that is down needs fear no fall,
He that is low no pride;
He that is humble ever shall
Have God to be his guide.

I am content with what I have,
Little be it or much;
And, Lord, contentment still I crave,
Because thou savest such.

Fullness to such a burden is
That go on pilgrimage;
Here little, and hereafter bliss,
Is best from age to age.

—JOHN BUNYAN

We know and rely on the love God has for us.
God is love. Whoever lives in love lives in God,
and God in him.

In this way, love is made complete among us
so that we will have confidence on the day of judgment,
because in this world we are like him.

We love because he first loved us.

1 John 4:16-17,19

TO BE *blessed* IS TO DISCOVER THAT GOD *cherishes* US MORE DEEPLY THAN WE DO OURSELVES. THIS *love* IS SO STRANGE AND OVERWHELMING THAT IT *transforms* OUR LIVES. IT LEAVES US NOT AS DIFFERENT PEOPLE, BUT AS OUR TRUE SELVES WITHOUT ANY OF THE PRETENSE. THUS, TO RECEIVE *God's blessing* IS TO COME HOME TO A PLACE WE HAVE NEVER BEEN, BUT KNOW WE BELONG THERE THE MOMENT WE ARRIVE. IT IS THE PLACE WHERE WE ARE UNCONDITIONALLY LOVED. THE *word* FOR *blessing* IN THE HEBREW IS ASHIR. IT MEANS TO FIND THE *right* PATH. AFTER SPENDING A LOT OF TIME ON THE WRONG PATHS,

YOU KNOW THAT THE *right* ONE WOULD LEAD YOU TO THIS GOD WHO *cherishes* YOU. WHEN JESUS USED THE WORD "BLESSED" IN THE BEATITUDES, HE CLAIMED THAT THE *right* PATH WAS THE OPPOSITE ONE FROM WHAT YOU EXPECTED. "BLESSED ARE THE POOR IN SPIRIT, FOR THEIRS IS THE *kingdom* OF HEAVEN…BLESSED ARE THE *meek,* FOR THEY WILL INHERIT THE EARTH" (MATTHEW 5:3,5). HE COULD ALSO HAVE SAID, "BLESSED ARE THE RECEIVERS, FOR THEY KNOW THEY ARE CHERISHED." THE RIGHT PATH ISN'T THE ROAD THAT WE CLIMB UP. IT IS THE ROAD THAT GOD CLIMBS DOWN TO *bless* US.

—M. CRAIG BARNES

*H*ow brightly beams the morning star!
What sudden radiance from afar

  Doth glad us with its shining?
Brightness of God, that breaks our night
And fills the darkened souls with light

  Who long for truth were pining!

   Rightly leads us,

   Life bestowing.
Praise, O praise such love o'erflowing!

Through thee alone can we be blest;
Then deep be on our hearts imprest

  The love that thou hast born us;
So make us ready to fulfill
With ardent zeal thy holy will,

  Though men may vex or scorn us;
Hold us, fold us, lest we fail thee.

   Lo, we hail thee,

   Long to know thee!
All we are and have we owe thee.

– J. A. Schlegel

The LORD gives strength to his people;
the LORD blesses his people with peace.

PSALM 29:11

Turn from evil and do good;
seek peace and pursue it.

PSALM 34:14

Consider the blameless, observe the upright;
there is a future for the man of peace.

PSALM 37:37

Jesus Christ is the same
yesterday and today and forever.

HEBREWS 13:8

*W*hen all seemed lost amid fiery trials, the most amazing thing happened. I found a hope in God that was independent of my hopes that he would do a particular thing. I realized that my hope was secure even though life was not. I had to live through those troubles, work through the pressing conflicts with others, grieve my lost dreams, and grow, slowly and painfully, into a more mature woman. But the sense of security I found in God's arms once I considered everything a loss was incredible. In giving up everything, there was nothing left to come between us.

—Connie Neal

Once we have received God's peace, we can go on to new adventures grounded in a tranquility that comes from him. If there have been huge mountains of discouragement in our lives, we now see that big obstacle is little more than a series of hills. We come to understand that we don't have to climb one big mountain without stopping. Rather we can take those smaller hills one at a time, ever climbing upward. As we are strengthened through the Lord's encouragement, it isn't long until we can look back and find we have just crossed the highest ridge.

*A*s for God, his way is perfect; the word of the LORD is flawless.
He is a shield for all who take refuge in him.
For who is God besides the LORD? And who is the Rock except our God?
It is God who arms me with strength and makes my way perfect.
He makes my feet like the feet of a deer; he enables me to stand on the heights.
He trains my hands for battle; my arms can bend a bow of bronze.
You give me your shield of victory; you stoop down to make me great.

2 Samuel 22:31–36

34

Chapter Three

ENCOURAGEMENT

QUIET TIMES FOR
Teachers

Awake, my soul, stretch every nerve,
And press with vigor on;
A heavenly race demands thy zeal,
And an immortal crown,
And an immortal crown.

A cloud of witnesses around
Hold thee in full survey;
Forget the steps already trod,
And onward urge thy way,
And onward urge thy way.

'Tis God's all animating voice
That calls thee from on high;
'Tis His own hand presents the prize
To thine aspiring eye.
Then wake, my soul, stretch every nerve,
And press with vigor on,
A heavenly race demands thy zeal,
And an immortal crown.

—PHILIP DODDRIDGE

Come, my children, listen to me;

I will teach you the fear of the LORD.

Whoever of you loves life

and desires to see many good days,

keep your tongue from evil

and your lips from speaking lies.

Turn from evil and do good;

seek peace and pursue it.

Psalm 34:11-14

*B*y night when others soundly slept
And hath at once both ease and Rest,
My waking eyes were open kept
And so to lie I found it best.

I sought him whom my Soul did Love,
With tears I sought him earnestly.
He bow'd his ear down from Above.
In vain I did not seek or cry.

My hungry Soul he fill'd with Good;
He in his Bottle put my tears,
My smarting wounds washt in his blood,
And banisht thence my Doubts and fears.

What to my Saviour shall I give
Who freely hath done this for me?
I'll serve him here whilst I shall live
And Love him to Eternity.

—Anne Bradstreet

The Sovereign LORD has given me an instructed tongue,

to know the word that sustains the weary.

He wakens me morning by morning,

wakens my ear to listen like one being taught.

The Sovereign LORD has opened my ears.

Isaiah 50:4–5

Instruct a wise man and he will be wiser still;

teach a righteous man and he will add to his learning.

"The fear of the LORD is the beginning of wisdom,

and knowledge of the Holy One is understanding."

Proverbs 9:9–10

There is a name I love to hear;
I love to sing its worth.
It sounds like music in mine ear,
The sweetest name on earth.

It tells me of a Savior's love,
Who died to set me free;
It tells me of His precious blood,
The sinner's perfect plea.

It tells me what my Father hath
In store for ev'ry day;
And tho' I tread a darksome path,
Yields sunshine all the way.

—FREDERICK WHITFIELD

40

THE LORD IS MY SHEPHERD,
I shall not be in want.
He makes me lie down in green pastures,
he leads me beside quiet waters,

he restores my soul.
He guides me in paths of righteousness
for his name's sake.

Even though I walk through the valley
of the shadow of death, I will fear no evil,
for you are with me; your rod and your staff,
they comfort me.

You prepare a table before me in the presence
of my enemies. You anoint my head with oil;
my cup overflows.

Surely goodness and love will follow me
all the days of my life, and I will dwell
in the house of the LORD forever.

Psalm 23:1–6

SING AND MAKE *music* IN YOUR HEART

TO THE LORD, ALWAYS GIVING *thanks*

TO GOD THE *Father* FOR EVERYTHING, IN
THE NAME OF OUR *Lord* JESUS CHRIST.

EPHESIANS 5:19–20

The way God works through his people is wild!

And the great thing is, he can use anyone.

Once you start praying, staying alert to the people

God sends into your life, God will begin to use you too.

You don't have to be in ministry. You don't have to be a full-

time evangelist. All you need is a willingness both to know

God better and make him known. But watch out.

When you start praying expectantly, be prepared—

because wild, even wonderful things will begin to happen.

—Becky Tirabassi

In the garden, in the garden of Jesus our Savior,

We are growing, we are growing for Jesus alone.

Like the flow'rs of the morning His garden adorning,

We are growing for Jesus, His loved and His own.

Little children, little children are the flow'rs in His garden,

We must blossom, we must blossom, for Jesus alone.

Jesus loves us, Jesus loves us, the flow'rs of His garden;

He will keep us, He will keep us, nor leave us alone.

We must love him, we must love Him, this Jesus our Savior,

We must trust Him, we must trust Him, in Jesus alone.

—Julia Harriet Johnson

My Heart Is Steadfast,

O God, my heart is steadfast;

I will sing and make music.

Awake, my soul! Awake, harp and lyre!

I will awaken the dawn.

I will praise you, O Lord, among the nations;

I will sing of you among the peoples.

For great is your love, reaching to the heavens;

your faithfulness reaches to the skies.

Be exalted, O God, above the heavens;

let your glory be over all the earth.

Psalm 57:7–11

Though we may feel enthusiastic
about doing great things for the Lord
in our chosen profession, there are times
when we are called to work for the Kingdom
of God by doing nothing—by waiting.
It may be that we are in a growth period
where we need to stretch our spiritual roots
a bit deeper…or enlarge our vision by learning
from others before we charge ahead to do
something for God. Our times of waiting in
patience can be treasured times, for it is then
that God drops a seed of understanding into
the soil of our soul. Though that seed may be
as small as a mustard seed, it can grow into a tree
that provides a huge umbrella of knowledge
to the young people we teach.

He will yet fill your mouth with laughter

and your lips with shouts of joy.

Job 8:21

You will find your joy in the LORD,

and I will cause you to ride on the heights of the land...

Surely the arm of the LORD is not too short to save,

nor his ear too dull to hear.

Isaiah 58:14—59:1

$\mathcal{I}$ would be true, for there are those who trust me.

I would be pure, for there are those who care.

I would be strong, for there is much to suffer.

I would be brave, for there is much to dare.

I would be friend of all—the foe, the friendless,

I would be giving, and forget the gift.

I would be humble, for I know my weakness.

I would look up, and laugh, and love, and lift.

I would be prayerful thro' each busy moment.

I would be constantly in touch with God.

I would be tuned to hear His slightest whisper.

I would have faith to keep the path Christ trod.

—Howard Arnold Walter
Author of third verse unknown

May our Lord Jesus Christ himself
and God our Father, who loved us
and by his grace gave us eternal encouragement
and good hope, encourage your hearts
and strengthen you in
every good deed and word.

May the Lord direct your hearts
into God's love and Christ's perseverance.

2 THESSALONIANS 2:16–17; 3:5

Prayer: LORD, PLEASE GIVE ME THE *courage* TO STAND UP FOR WHAT IS RIGHT NO MATTER *what* IT COSTS.

*I*f we hope for what we do not yet have, we wait for it patiently.

In the same way, the Spirit helps us in our weakness. We do not know what we ought to pray for, but the Spirit himself intercedes for us with groans that words cannot express. And he who searches our hearts knows the mind of the Spirit, because the Spirit intercedes for the saints in accordance with God's will.

We know that in all things God works for the good of those who love him.

Romans 8:25-28

Reassure ME THAT AS I DO THIS,

YOU WILL MAKE ME A *person* WHO IS

TRULY *free* AND FULL OF JOY.

—ANN SPANGLER

*We will often suffer loss, fear,
confusion, and pain in our quest
to be faithful to what and whom
we believe in. But as we trust God
for the outcome, we will experience
a new freedom. Perhaps an angel
will even stand by our side and
in the midst or our distress,
unbinding and protecting us
from the devouring flames that
threaten to consume us.*

Patience is not the same thing as resignation

or the cynical attitude that always expects the worst

possible outcome. Patience is a more positive trait.

It is the ability to bear affliction, delay and interruption

with calmness, perseverance and confidence in the goodness

of God. It is inward peace as well as outward control.

It is the submission of our schedules, our viewpoints,

our dreams to the greater plan of God, with the conviction

that he has a good reason for every delay he allows

to come our way.

— Barbara Bush

Therefore, since we are surrounded

by such a great cloud of witnesses,

let us throw off everything that hinders

and the sin that so easily entangles,

and let us run with perseverance the race

marked out for us. Let us fix our eyes on Jesus,

the author and perfecter of our faith,

Hebrews 12:1–2

Jesus said, "Surely I am with you always,

to the very end of the age."

Matthew 28:20

Germ of new life, whose powers expanding slow

For many a moon their full perfection wait,—

Haste, precious pledge of happy love, to go

Auspicious borne through life's mysterious gate.

What powers lie folded in thy curious frame,—

Senses from objects locked, and mind from thought!

How little canst thou guess thy lofty claim

To grasp at all the worlds the Almighty wrought!

—Anna Lætitia Barbauld

Jesus replied, "If anyone loves me,
he will obey my teaching.
My Father will love him,
and we will come to him
and make our home with him."

John 14:23

For God so loved the world
that he gave his one and only Son,
that whoever believes
in him shall not perish
but have eternal life.

John 3:16

*W*HEN WE HAVE LEARNED to rest in patience,
we find our eyes more fully open to know
and accept God's Word and apply it to our lives.
We find his wisdom everywhere. We find it in
our daily living. Practical things that we never
imagined could take on a spiritual meaning—
suddenly do. In them, we see eternal concepts
and doctrines the Bible teaches. These all become
a personal letter from God that both lifts us up to
see his perspective on the great matters of the universe,
and causes us to fall to our knees and humbly regard
the tiniest flower as his masterpiece of creation.

Chapter Five

PERSPECTIVE

At age twenty-nine, I was struck down

with the undignified curse of chicken pox.

God's sense of humor? His perfect timing?

Only one reason has ever kept my itinerant

husband at home in bed for more than a day or two,

and that is a recurring back problem. Sure enough,

those back muscles collapsed during the second week

I was confined to bed. We couldn't walk away from

each other, as we had been doing for so long.

We were forced to talk to each other—

for a whole week! The God of righteousness

and holiness was at work. The God of love

was healing our marriage. I was beginning

to understand true security in the assurance

of my Creator's love.

– Joy Jacobs

Commit to the LORD whatever you do,
and your plans will succeed.
The LORD works out everything for his own ends.
In his heart a man plans his course,
but the LORD determines his steps.
How much better to get wisdom than gold,
to choose understanding rather than silver!

PROVERBS 16:3–4,9,16

TIME IS THE MEASURE BUT OF CHANGE;
No present hour is found;

The past, the future, fill the range

Of Time's unceasing round.

Where then is now?

In realms above,

With God's atoning Lamb

In regions of eternal love,

Where sits enthroned I AM.

Then pilgrim, let thy joys and tears

On Time no longer lean;

But henceforth all thy homes and fears

From earth's affections wean:

To God let votive accents rise;

With truth, with virtue, live;

So all the bliss that Time denies

Eternity shall give.

—John Quincy Adams,
sixth President of the United States

For we are God's workmanship,
created in Christ Jesus to do good works,
which God prepared in advance for us to do.

Ephesians 2:10

One last fear I had to face and deal
with in order to reestablish freedom
in my life was the fear of failure.
God knows I'm dealing with a whole
bunch of deficits. God still loved me
as much when I couldn't perform
as he did when I performed brilliantly.
I came to realize that I am destined
to fail sometimes, but since I am seeking
to love God, he isn't going to punish me
every time I show my frailty or lack of
understanding. He may take me through
experiences that help me learn to understand.

– Jan Dravecky

Whoever gives heed to instruction prospers,
and blessed is he who trusts in the LORD.
The wise in heart are called discerning,
and pleasant words promote instruction.
Understanding is a fountain
of life to those who have it,
but folly brings punishment to fools.
A wise man's heart guides his mouth,
and his lips promote instruction.
Pleasant words are a honeycomb,
sweet to the soul and healing to the bones.

PROVERBS 16:20–24

Now what harm will befall you
in taking the side of faith in God?
You will be faithful, honest, humble,
grateful, generous, a sincere friend,
and truthful. I tell you what you will
thereby gain in this life, and that,
at each step you take on this road you
will see so great certainty of gain, so much
nothingness in what you risk, that you will
at last recognize that you have wagered
for something certain and infinite,
for which you have given nothing.

If this discourse pleases you and seems
impressive, know that it is made by a man
who has knelt, both before and after it,
in prayer to that Being, infinite and without
parts, before whom he lays all he has,
for you also to lay before Him all you have
for your own good and for His glory,
so that strength may be given to lowliness.

— Blaise Pascal

So then, just as you received Christ Jesus as Lord,
continue to live in him, rooted and built up in him,
strengthened in the faith as you were taught.

Colossians 2:6–7

strengthened
in faith

In prayer, we are confronted
with the important difference between
doing works for God, and doing the work of God.
In this sense, it is not like a building project,
so much as a garden. God has designed flowers
and vegetables to grow by a life
that we cannot control. But we can learn how to
cooperate with God by discerning how to create
a productive garden. To do this, we have to learn
how to grow things according to the plan of God,
which he placed in the structure of each seed.

—BRAD LONG

Create in me a pure heart, O God,

and renew a steadfast spirit within me…

Restore to me the joy of your salvation

and grant me a willing spirit, to sustain me.

Then I will teach transgressors your ways,

and sinners will turn back to you…

My tongue will sing of your righteousness.

O Lord, open my lips,

and my mouth will declare your praise.

Psalm 51:10,12–15

Prayer: LORD JESUS, I AM WHO I AM BY YOUR *loving* DESIGN. HELP ME TO ACCEPT MY WEAKNESSES AS WELL AS MY *strengths.*

It has taken me some time to come to terms with the fact that I simply do not, never did, and never will feel comfortable in the presence of a number. I do, however, provide endless merriment for my friends as I valiantly try to calculate the tip from a lunch tab…I have finally embraced my deficit with a reluctant warmth. After all, there's something to be said for consistent inability: It makes others feel secure.

—*Marilyn Meberg*

HELP ME, TOO, TO *embrace* MYSELF IN MY

totality AS YOU EMBRACE ME.

—MARILYN MEBERG

*H*ow great is the love the Father has lavished on us,
that we should be called children of God! And that is
what we are! The reason the world does not know us
is that it did not know him. Dear friends, now we are
children of God, and what we will be has not yet been
made known. But we know that when he appears,
we shall be like him, for we shall see him as he is.

1 John 3:1–2

In God's economy, everything is reversed:
Weakness is strength. The last shall be first.
The foolish things of the world God uses to
confound the wise. The meek inherit the earth.

How many times do the words and actions
need to be said and done before we see the picture,
understand the message, and obey the commands?

—Cal Thomas

last shall
be first

*J*ESUS BEGAN TO TEACH THEM, SAYING:

"Blessed are the poor in spirit,
for theirs is the kingdom of heaven.

Blessed are those who mourn,
for they will be comforted.

Blessed are the meek,
for they will inherit the earth.

Blessed are those who hunger
and thirst for righteousness,
for they will be filled.

Blessed are the merciful,
for they will be shown mercy.

Blessed are the pure in heart,
for they will see God.

Blessed are the peacemakers,
for they will be called sons of God."

Matthew 5:2–9

When the subject of thankfulness is introduced,

the once-a-year tradition of "counting our blessings"

on Thanksgiving Day may come to mind.

But Biblical thankfulness is more than just being

grateful for the good things that happen in our lives.

It includes understanding God's perspective on what a

"blessing" is in the first place. We think of blessings as

the good things that happen to us. God has a wider view

of our lives than we do, and when we accept his wider

view and keep the eternal ends in mind, we come to a

place where we can be thankful even for difficult

experiences that commonly wouldn't be thought

of as blessings.

Chapter Six

THANKFULNESS

I ♥ my teacher

QUIET TIMES FOR
Teachers

How can we have thankful, contented hearts
when the circumstances in our lives are not what
we had planned and when they lie outside
our control or our power to change?

Let's look at our alternatives. If we are not thankful,
we become bitter and angry with God: he is not providing
what we "rightfully" deserve. If we are not content,
we become rebellious and complaining.

God's love for his people is not determined by the
circumstances in our lives. His love is steadfast.
The same God who formed the world in six days,
knows every hair on our heads…sent his Son to die
on the cross to redeem us from our sins.

Our marital status, career or finances might fluctuate
or totally break apart. In spite of that, however,
we can and must give him thanks for his love toward us.
We must serve him with unhesitating hearts.

– Carol L. Baldwin

Praise the LORD, all you nations;
extol him, all you peoples.
For great is his love toward us,
and the faithfulness of the LORD endures
forever.

PSALM 117:1–2

WE CANNOT *kindle* WHEN WE WILL THE FIRE WHICH IN

THE *heart* RESIDES; THE *spirit* BLOWETH AND IS STILL,

IN MYSTERY OUR *soul* ABIDES. BUT TASKS IN HOURS OF

INSIGHT WILL'D CAN BE THROUGH HOURS OF GLOOM

FULFILL'D. WHEN THOU DOST BASK IN NATURE'S EYE,

ASK, HOW SHE VIEW'D THY SELF-CONTROL,

THY STRUGGLING, TASK'D *morality*— NATURE,

WHOSE FREE, LIGHT, *cheerful* AIR, OFT MADE THEE,

IN THY GLOOM, DESPAIR. AND SHE,

Show my your ways, O LORD,
    teach me your paths;

guide me in your truth and teach me,
    for you are God my Savior,
    and my hope is in you all day long.

Remember, O LORD, your great mercy and love,
    for they are from of old.

Remember not the sins of my youth
    and my rebellious ways;

WHOSE CENSURE THOU DOSTDREAD, WHOSE EYE

THOU WAST AFRAID TO SEEK, SEE, ON HER FACE

A *glow* IS SPREAD, A STRONG EMOTION ON HER

CHEEK! "AH, CHILD!" SHE CRIES, "THAT STRIFE DIVINE,

WHENCE WAS IT, FOR IT IS NOT MINE?" THERE IS NO

EFFORT ON MY BROW— I DO NOT *strive,* I DO NOT

WEEP; I RUSH WITH THE SWIFT SPHERES AND *glow*

IN JOY, AND WHEN I WILL, I *sleep.*

—MATTHEW ARNOLD

according to your love remember me,
for you are good, O LORD.

Good and upright is the LORD;
therefore he instructs sinners in his ways.

He guides the humble in what is right
and teaches them his way.

All the ways of the LORD are loving and faithful
for those who keep the demands of his covenant.

Psalm 25:5–10

I KNOW THAT MY REDEEMER LIVES;

What joy that blest assurance gives!

He lives, he lives who once was dead;

He lives, my everlasting head.

He lives to bless me with his love,

And still he pleads for me above;

He lives to raise me from the grave,

And me eternally to save.

—*Samuel Medley*

I will sing of the LORD's great love forever;

    with my mouth I will make

        your faithfulness known through all generations.

I will declare that your love stands firm forever,

    that you established your faithfulness in heaven itself…

The heavens praise your wonders, O LORD,

    your faithfulness too, in the assembly of the holy ones.

For who in the skies above can compare with the LORD?

    Who is like the LORD among the heavenly beings?

Psalm 89:1–2,5–6

raise your wonders

*T*he core of God's plan is to rescue us
from our sin. Our pain, poverty,
and broken hearts are not his ultimate focus.
He cares about them, but they are merely symptoms
of the real problem. Every sorrow we taste will
one day prove to be the best possible thing that
could have happened. We will thank God endlessly
in heaven for the trials he sent to us here.

No speculative religious philosophy dreamed up
in my head, no belief in a vague and all-supreme
First Cause, no creed about God could sustain
and give me peace in this chair. And certainly such
things could not actually make me rejoice in my
condition. There is a living God behind all of this
who is more than just a theological axiom.
He is personal, and He works and proves
Himself in my life.

– *Joni Eareckson Tada*

There is no one like the God of Jeshurun,
who rides on the heavens to help you
and on the clouds in his majesty.

The eternal God is your refuge,
and underneath are the everlasting arms.
Who is like you, a people saved by the LORD?

He is your shield and helper
and your glorious sword.

DEUTERONOMY 33:26-27,29

O worship the King

All glorious above;

And gratefully sing

His power and his love:

Our shield and defender,

The ancient of days,

Pavilioned in splendour,

And girded with praise.

O tell of his might,

O sing of his grace,

Whose robe is the light,

Whose canopy space.

—*Sir Robert Grant*

I WILL EXTOL THE LORD AT ALL TIMES;
    his praise will always be on my lips.
My soul will boast in the LORD;
    let the afflicted hear and rejoice.

Glorify the LORD with me;
    let us exalt his name together.

I sought the LORD, and he answered me;
    he delivered me from all my fears.

Those who look to him are radiant;
    their faces are never covered with shame.

Taste and see that the LORD is good;
    blessed is the man who takes refuge in him.

Psalm 34:1–5,8

Your faith will be increased as you catch a glimpse
of the glory of heaven and of the host of God's angels.
Joy and confidence will spring up in your heart as
you realize that the ultimate supernatural event
will be our resurrection to everlasting life with
Christ in a place where there will be no more tears,
pain, nor tragedy.

See His glory before you! Hear the songs of praises
being sung! Hear the great choirs of angels as they sing:
"To him who sits on the throne and to the Lamb be
praise and honor and glory and power, for ever and ever!"
(Revelation 5:13).

—*Hope MacDonald*

From the lips of children
and infants you have ordained praise…

When I consider your heavens,
the work of your fingers,
the moon and the stars,
which you have set in place,

what is man that you are mindful of him,
the son of man that you care for him?

You made him a little lower than
the heavenly beings and crowned him
with glory and honor.

O LORD, our Lord, how majestic is
your name in all the earth!

Psalm 8:2–5,9

OFTEN, AT DUSK, when the sun and clouds
are placed just so, they create the color
of a flower vendor's rose, and I remember
how it feels to be twenty-three years old.

When we place, side by side, who we are today
with who we were yesterday, we make comparisons.
It is clear that, like the moon, we reflect the light
of that which glows before us: those we have loved,
where we have been, and what we had once hoped
to accomplish, and in such reflection we can see
a difference.

I believe that people who have been collecting bits
of goodness along the way will like what they see
as they pass before the mirror of eternity.

—Christopher de Vinck

Every good and perfect gift is from above,

coming down from the Father of the heavenly lights,

who does not change like shifting shadows.

James 1:17

God WILL SEND ALL KINDS OF BLESSINGS. AND ALL HIS *blessings* GO TOGETHER LIKE LINKS IN A GOLDEN CHAIN. IF HE *gives* YOU SAVING *grace,* HE WILL ALSO GIVE YOU COMFORTING GRACE. GOD WILL SEND "SHOWERS OF BLESSINGS."

LOOK UP TODAY, *you* WHO ARE DRIED AND *withered* PLANTS. OPEN YOUR *leaves* AND FLOWERS AND *receive* GOD'S HEAVENLY *watering.*

—CHARLES H. SPURGEON

I will make a covenant of peace with them and rid the land of wild beasts so that they may live in the desert and sleep in the forests in safety.

I will bless them and the places surrounding my hill. I will send down showers in season; there will be showers of blessing.

The trees of the field will yield their fruit and the ground will yield its crops; the people will be secure in their land. They will know that I am the Lord, when I break the bars of their yoke and rescue them from the hands of those who enslaved them.

Ezekiel 34:25–27

We worship not only on our knees
but also as we live our lives.
Our everyday lives are important to God,
important enough that he sent his Son
to die on the cross so that Jesus could live
in us through each day —
including the ordinary ones.

We can now say:
"I'm going to school to worship God."
"I'm going to paint a picture to worship God."
"I'm going to clean the kitchen to worship God."
"I'm going to my job to worship God."
as well as
"I'm going to church to worship God."

—MARIE CHAPIAN

Therefore, I urge you, brothers,

in view of God's mercy,

to offer your bodies as living sacrifices,

holy and pleasing to God—

this is your spiritual act of worship.

Do not conform any longer to the pattern

of this world, but be transformed

by the renewing of your mind.

Then you will be able to test and approve

what God's will is—his good,

pleasing and perfect will.

Romans 12:1-2

Follow the way of love.

1 Corinthians 14:1

SOURCES

Baldwin, Carol L. *Women's Devotional Bible.* Grand Rapids: ZondervanPublishingHouse, 1990.

Barnes, M. Craig. *Hustling God: Why We Work So Hard for What God Wants to Give.* Grand Rapids: ZondervanPublishingHouse, 1999.

Bush, Barbara. *Heart Trouble.* Grand Rapids: ZondervanPublishingHouse, 1981.

Chapian, Marie. *Women's Devotional Bible.* Grand Rapids: ZondervanPublishingHouse, 1990.

Dravecky, Jan. *A Joy I'd Never Known.* Grand Rapids: ZondervanPublishingHouse, 1996.

Jacobs, Joy. *When God Seems Far Away.* Dillsburg, PA: Daybreak Ministries, 1993.

Long, Brad. *Prayer That Shapes the Future.* Grand Rapids: ZondervanPublishingHouse, 1998.

MacDonald, Hope. *When Angels Appear.* Grand Rapids: ZondervanPublishingHouse, 1982.

Meberg, Marilyn. *Joybreaks.* Grand Rapids: ZondervanPublishingHouse, 1997.

Neal, Connie. *Dancing In the Arms of God.* Grand Rapids: ZondervanPublishingHouse, 1995.

Spangler, Ann. *An Angel a Day: Stories of Angelic Encounters.* Grand Rapids: ZondervanPublishingHouse, 1994.

Shaw, Luci. *Water My Soul.* Grand Rapids: ZondervanPublishingHouse, 1998.

Tada, Joni Eareckson. *A Step Further.* Grand Rapids: ZondervanPublishingHouse, 1978.

Tada, Joni Eareckson. *When God Weeps.* Grand Rapids: ZondervanPublishingHouse, 1998.

Thomas, Cal. *Blinded By Might.* Grand Rapids: ZondervanPublishingHouse, 1998.

Tirabassi, Becky. *Wild Things Happen When I Pray.* Grand Rapids: ZondervanPublishingHouse, 1994.

de Vinck, Christopher. *The Book of Moonlight.* Grand Rapids: ZondervanPublishingHouse, 1998.

Walsh, Sheila. *Faith, Hope, Love: Scripture and Lyrics to Bring Joy to Your Heart and Peace to Your Soul.* Grand Rapids: ZondervanPublishingHouse, 1998.